Vendors Jubilee Magazine

Copyright © 2018 Life Empowerment Publishing

All rights reserved.

ISBN-13: **978-1724832016**

ISBN-10: 1724832018

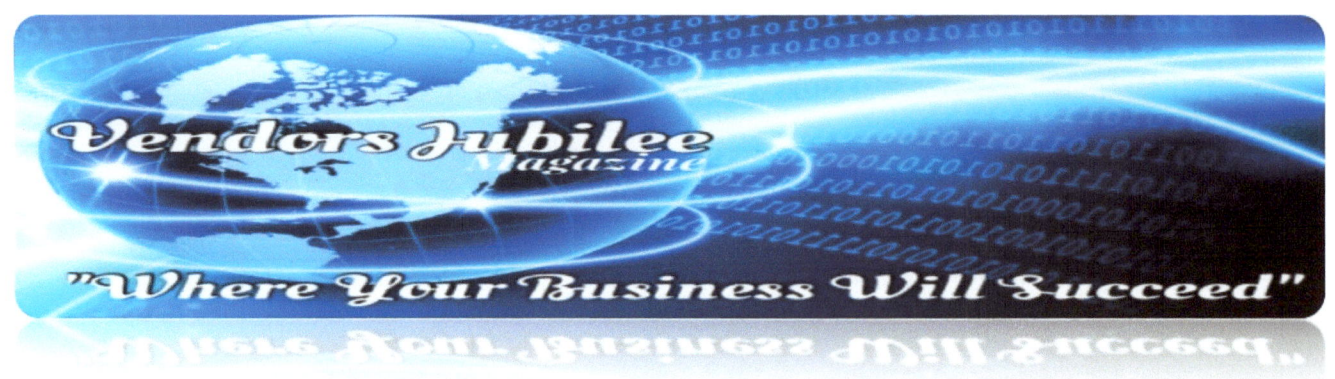

Just -Understanding-Business-In-Life-Everyday-Events

Mission/Vision:

To help aid in accomplishing entrepreneur's growth within their business establishment. To help consumers to purchase, join and applying Kingdom building to edify growth within our communities, cities, and states.

Shamika Curry founder CEO, Vendors Jubilee, along with her husband Joseph M. Curry

Vendors Jubilee was founded in 2016 location Jacksonville Florida and now resides in Fairview Heights Illinois. Our Global establishment is design with entrepreneurs like yourself in mind, to help aid and establish growth within your business. It's our company delight to assist your business to success with a high-volume flow of customers to your business establishment. It's our business to make sure your business succeeds.

We believe, at Vendors Jubilee your business will Succeed!

Mrs. Shamika Curry
Founder CEO

Dear Valued Customer

Vendors Jubilee Magazine is delighted, you decided to market your business "Better Wear Custom Apparel."

Our magazine was created to help aid in entrepreneurs' growth within their business establishment. Every, business owner, vendors, communities, church, and conference events are structure to establish consumers to purchase, join, and apply Kingdom building to edify growth within our communities, cities and states. This magazine issue will be distributed quarterly.

This is a global magazine, will be available on amazon, other online merchant stores, local boutiques, doctors' offices, beauty salons in Metro East and St Louis Mo area. Just to name a couple other states Georgia, Florida, Texas, and many more.

Your ad will be available throughout the years. Please send your ad information to: vendorsjubileemagazine@gmail.com

www.vendorsjubilee.com

Thank you for your support, we can impact the world with economic growth within our communities for God's Glory!

We honor and appreciate our customers!

Thank you,

Mrs. Shamika Curry
Founder CEO
Pastor Joseph Curry
Editor- In- Chief
Vendors Jubilee Magazine

Contents

Donta Moore
Producer Editor
"Light the Dark"
Tell his Story

8

35

Dr. Nikki Weiss

Healthy & Wealthy

Sean Thomas
Scooda
Tells his Story

13-14

36

Pastor Joseph M. Curry
Man with a Vision
"Locker Room The Movie"

18

Deandre Thompson
Father Crop
"Cream of the Crop"

22-24

43

Bless it Up!
Bless.Co
Clothing Line

William Davis
Ceo

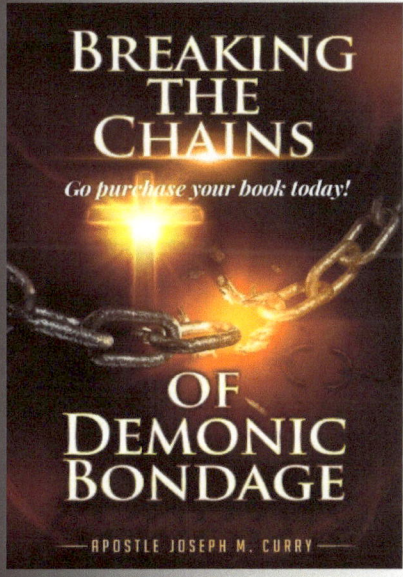

Order Your Books Today!

www.amazon.com

CASTING CALL
MYSTIQUEE AGENCY

ATLANTA GEORGIA
SEND BIO TO
LIFEEMPOWERMENTFILMS@GMAIL.COM

DATE AND LOCATION
TBA

AUDITIONS

Donta Moore

Light The Dark"

Donta Moore is a native of St. Louis Missouri, married to Brittany Moore; they are the proud parents of five children, ages two month through eleven years of age. He is an editor, producer, song engineer, mix and master person, also do video photography. At the age of five he started his love and writing music, but it was more secular music. In 2005 he taken a liken to Christian hip hop music, is when he was introduced to Christian hip hop artist, like Lecrae, and The Truth, so he knew he like and can do Christian hip hop music. At the age of eleven he was kidnap and it last for an hour getting pistol whip and all other situation, but through the grace of God he keeps me and brought me out of this situation. So, I try to reach the youth and group of peoples through my music. He said," he wants to bring more positive music and films to our communities.

So, he did a few performances, when attending a Job Corps in Kansas City Mo, when he meets a young man who was into gospel hip hop too at the age fourteen.

The name of his music is LTD "Light the Dark" he went from secular music to Christian hip hop. He always took liken to more conscious rap making good music all around without having to use profanity and more clean-cut music. Even if we are talking about violence all around us we are talking more about positive music that will create hope for Gods people.

Now at the age of thirty, his goals in the next five years is to have a record label to be able to create good music again, this generation has kind lost their love and value for music. He wants to create more positive way for good music to change the environment in a more positive way to give back to our community.

He is now working on some new projects, sound track for Locker Room the

Movie and LTD five more projects coming soon!

He said his friends will say he is an honest. keep promises. very humble loyal person.

His dream he wants to accomplish is filming even though he is into music, but he also found his love and passion for film. So, He started to invest in buying camera to fulfill his new-found love for filming, he said he think he love filming more than music, and he is always looking for opportunity to put his skills to work.

He said the quality of film and music is what he looks for that inspire him to want to give more quality to his work. Watching different movies see their lightening and quality they brought to this film. This has inspired him to want to give great quality film to movies, through his music and filming, he wants to tell his story. Any one who will listen to music, or just read his story to never give up on your dream keep pressing forward and trusting in God he will make your dreams come to past.

Contact Donta Moore @ 1 (314)782-0228

"Gifted Hands Mime Ministry"

Stacy Davis native of East St. Louis IL married to Charlese Davis and they have four children ages eight month through four years of age. He is the founder of Gifted Hands Mime Ministry. He started his love for mime ministry in 2007 at the Master Baptist Convention in St Louis Mo, it was either sing in the choir or learn how to dance, so he joined the mime dance ministry, under the leadership of Minister Kenny Rodger, so he fell in love with it, and started pursuing mime dance at the age of thirteen.

He started Gifted Hands Mime Ministry, this name came about because, he always using his hands. He said he knew he is gifted and the anointing of God is in his hands.

He then started mentoring youth under Gifted Hands Mime Ministry for Mrs. Janet Greenly Mentor with Purpose, since then He has been teaching mime ministry for nine years. It was a great opportunity to teach youth mime dance.

He has been going to church all his life, he was forced to be an usher and, on the choir, but he loved mime dance ministry. When it came to mime dance he knew in his heart this was the Ministry he wanted to teach youth. He said, to see the kid put on their white faces and gloves brought a smile on his face, just to see them minister to God people and loved dancing too. This really motivates him to mentor the youth, keeping them out of trouble and giving them more out of life to look forward too.

His goals in the next five years he wants to expand to open a facility, to teaching more, not only mime dance, but basketball, teach them how to count money, mentor them in everyday practical living.

Gifted Hands Ministry is also working on a play with Mentor with Purpose,

"Crack but not Broken" this is a church play for our local community in East St. Louis IL.

He wants to start a mentorship community program center in the city of East St. Louis IL, offering different programs, more than dancing, to keep our children off the street and stop the killing in this area.

He said his friends would say he is a down to earth guy, who always honest keep everyone out of trouble and a dependable friend.

His inspiration comes from these men of God who inspired him, because they work in the community and gave back to the community and the were hard-working men. Pastor Johnny Robertson, his grandfather Willie Wood, and his brother Dug Riley. They keep young men off the street and his Pastor from New Life Community Church, Pastor Kenndall Granger.

Booking : giftedhands2015.jr@gmail.com

GHMM 314 226-8824

"You are a Student of Life for Life"

Minister Pierre Lott is a native of East St Louis IL, he is apart "Bird Mode Family".

He said music has always been a part of his life since age thirteen, from playing the drum, trumpet, trombone, and keyboard. At the age of twenty, he started to produce music and his cousin introduce him to a music software called Fruity loop FSL Studio. He has been written poetry and rapping for over twenty years.

He started it as a ministry in 2010, ever since then God has been blessing him with opportunity. He started with a group called Bird Mode Evangelical music group is a body of recording artist. Deandre Thompson "Father Crop" is the founder Ceo and Laborers Rapp group, Kenta Sincere" Donta Moore" Christian hip hop family ministry including himself. He got saved at the age sixteen with no understanding on how salvation work. He had to get an understanding what is means to be Christian first, then to be a minister, getting an understand on what is mean to be a Christian, he rededicated his life at age twenty one with more knowledge and understanding what is faith, grace and mercy and how much through having a relationship with God, through grace and mercy, of his salvation and learned more from his former Pastor Lamarce Tart " Living Word Fellowship", in East St. Louis IL.

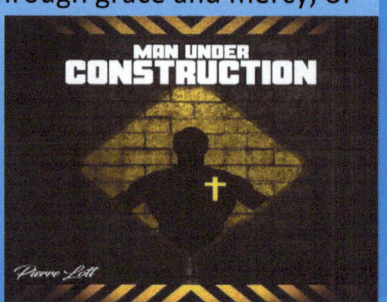

In the next five years he sees himself doing music in ministry fulltime and taking music global to help produce other music rap artists and continue to accomplish to inspire people to live the life that is given to them, to better understand what God has called them too. He is now thirty-three years of age; he is now working on a project call "Men Under Construction" and "The other side of Love" with the Bird Mode Family.

Wanting to help and be an inspirational leader. His friend will say he is a humble, loyal, go getter, weird, success driven fun down to earth cool to be around type of guy. Beside being a recording artist and poet, he wants to operate in an excellence spirit, being a student of life for life.

He said being a musician and an artist and creative ideas inspires him. He is always inspire to find out new and different thing to want to help make things better. He also wants to be an inspiration to all God children that is made in His image and likeness, to know God more and understand who He is in their life.

He also started listens to other Christian rappers to get more of understanding on how rap music can be use as tool for ministry and not just for money and fame, so he started to listen to Cross Movement, Flame, Lecrae, Truth, R-Swift and many more others.

He begins to learn sound doctrine and study the word, to show his self-approve, so he can have more knowledge on how to implement rap music as a ministry tool to reach out to Gods people. He started rapping in ministry at the age of twenty-five.

He wrote his first gospel song, and it open the door up to meet new gospel artists, Deandre Thompson, Brother Dre, Larry Rodgers, and many more, in the East St. Louis and St. Louis regions. God has guide him through it all and I he is so grateful for what God has done for him in his life and ministry.

"You are a Student of Life for Life"

TRUST IN THE BLOOD

By Pierre Lott

"Blood Is Thicker than Water" is the most used statement that family members use to teach the young ones that "friends may come and go, but families are forever".

However, I got a friend that stick closer than a brother.

In fact, I got a few friends that I call "brothers, because they were born for adversity.

Nothing against my brother, but almost every story that is about brotherhood ends in blood shedding.

So, what is so great about a bloodstain that can't be removed?

I was told that Christ had to rip the veil, because there were bad blood between us like sickle cell. Anemia.

Well, I guess that was the nectar of the fruit from that tree, because Adam and Eve became vampires for a moment.

With a state of mind that is not of this world, I have learned to keep my friends close and my families closer, because anybody can be my enemies.

So, who or what shall I trust when it comes to my protection?

What shall cover me in order for those who sit on the seat of scornful to not touch?

What can purge me from being the old me into becoming the "Me" that I didn't know of, yet those who never took the time to know me are too lazy to catch up?

What can wash away my sin even when my sin was once another part of me?
MJ.

TRUST IN THE BLOOD

I asked the Lord, "Can I be baptized in your vein and don't pull me out until I make it to your heart?"

It seems like one drop of his blood is enough to put me under witness protection.

Better than the mark of Cain.

Cleanse from my insane paranoia in my brain.

Now, I can be quick to think.

Have the confidence to walk through the valley of the shadow of death and fear no evil.

Speak the words of a wise man who fulfilled a legend that was meant for him to reveal.

And it is amazing that many are still trying to clothe their nakedness of wrongdoings with justification.

While our Savior took his cross and turned the place of skull into a blood clinic.

Donating salvation to those who needs a transfusion.

In that case, Lord, create in me a clean heart.

Renew a right spirit.

Change my ways and identity with your DNA.

And let whatever overflows be what you say.

If I had to choose between life and death,

I choose the one that leads me to trust…in…the BLOOD!

Scooda

"Music is a Tool for Christ"

Sean Thomas is thirty years of age, he is a native of St Louis Missouri, married to Nisie Thomas together they have five children, their youngest child nine months. He is a radio host, rap artist, and a evangelist, his love for music started at the age of eleven years of age. At the young age of nine, he did not know he can do Christian rap music until he heard this guy by the name, "Praiz" Vace Watt from St. Louis Mo. He made a rap jingle, he was a Christian rapper. So, he was inspired to do rap. He started to hear rap music at the age of nine years old, that's when his eyes and ear was open. He started to see artist doing Hip Hop Christian rap. At the age thirteen he started to write gospel rap. His first experience started at his church, they were doing a youth rally, and a couple of his friend from the church got together was like let's do some Christian rap. I did not believe it was popular are even can be done, because I haven't done any research on it. We tried the Christian rap at the youth rally that night and I really liked the music, it was something about that night, and every since the youth rally at his church that night he begins to really like Christian rap and keep it going. He wanted to use it as a tool to evangelize to God people, being a preacher kid, his mother is an evangelist.

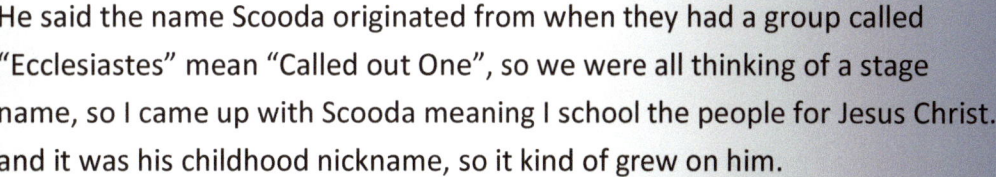

He said the name Scooda originated from when they had a group called "Ecclesiastes" mean "Called out One", so we were all thinking of a stage name, so I came up with Scooda meaning I school the people for Jesus Christ. and it was his childhood nickname, so it kind of grew on him.

Having a personal relationship with Christ, has given him so much love for God people, because of the love he has for Christ and growing in Love with Christ help him love others. he is a husband, father and active in his church, he applies those same principle to his life and toward his family and Gods people. He said he loves doing music and want to share the love of God with others through music, because music is powerful and it's a tool to be able to minister to God people, so why not us music as a tool. He started a podcast and said why not do this for Christ, so he started interviewing a lot of artists, and doing it for the gospel. Being a radio personality, he must have love for Gods people, he wanted to use his gift God has given him to reach people through music. His mother was a radio personality host, being in the studio with her, really inspire him to want to do radio. He said ,he love radio and music it is fun, that he can minister to God people, while having fun and people are getting healed and delivered at the same time.

It feels great to hear people say, listening to your songs or radio show really blessed me, it really feels great knowing you are being use by God, and people are being restore back to God, really feels awesome!

He said, his goal in the next five years, he wants to stop working a nine to five, travel with minister, be able to take care of his family and work full time in ministry to allow God to pour into him, so he can pour back into God people.

His new project he is working on music is a mix tape, he been doing music for year and he have not release an album or CDs yet, so he need to finish this project doing his songs putting them on a track, so it will be available at the end of 2018. He is also working on a new project for radio so stay tune.

Scooda said a lot of his friends will say he is goofy and really fun to hang around, hey said he should be a comedy instead of a rapper. He is really a people person he is really a cool dude. He always wants to make people smile. He said laughter Is good for your heart.

Outside music and radio, he works as hospitality guest agent at a hotel. You must be a people person and discernment to know if someone hurting. Working at customer service really help me to be able to engage with God people in the audience when minister in music.

His wife really inspires him, she is a strong and independent woman, she is very goal oriented, helps him manage life by keeping things balance in their life.

For the love of music, let music be a tool to get the word out for Christ!

Anybody out there, stay encourage and keep pushing

Proverbs 18:16 (KJV)

A man's gift maketh room for him, and bringeth him before great men.

John 12;32 (NIV)

And I, when I am lifted up from the earth, will draw all people to myself

"Anybody out there, stay encourage and keep pushing "

Radio Personality/Christian Hip Hop/Event Host

www.iamscooda.com

Host of the Scooda Radio Show on

KATZ Hallelujah 1600AM

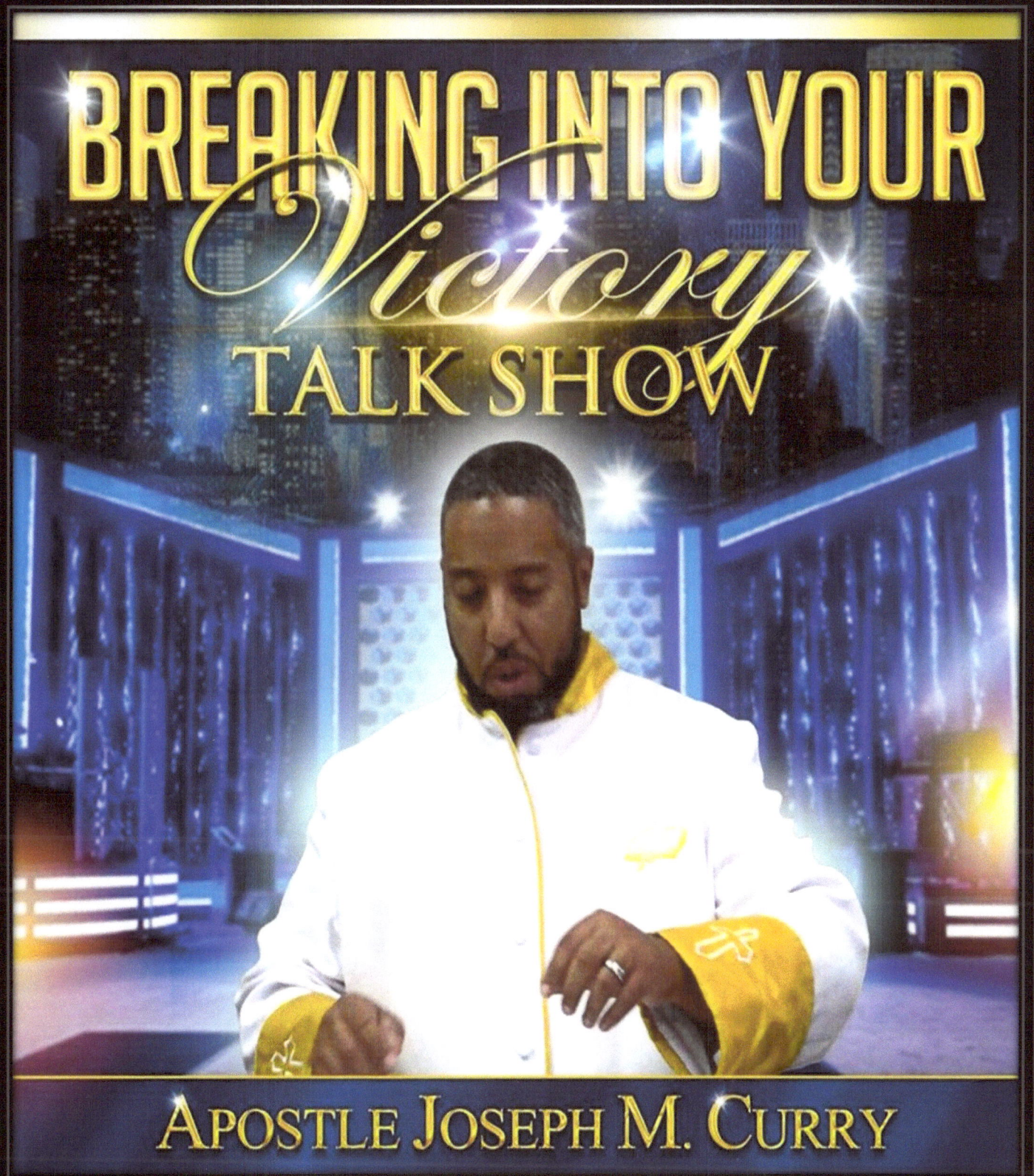

Saving your Marriage

3 tips on how to save your marriage
- Pray
- Communicate
- Date

Pastor Joseph & Shamika Curry

Remember before you can save your marriage, you must acknowledge there is a problem.

3 TIPS

- Praying together is a very great way to save your marriage, as you two agree together God will work out whatever you have petition before Him. Matthew 18:20

- Communication is the key to saving your marriage, because it allows you to express your feeling, giving the other partner an opportunity to listen. Psalm 37:30

- Dating each other on a regular bases will save your marriage, planning trips, going on couiples retreats, are just a dinner and movie at home or outings. Amos 3:3

Food for thought

Remember God is Love, so treat your spouse the way you would treat God! I John 4:7-21

Need prayer Contact :

Pastors Joseph & Shamika Curry

www.worldharvestfaith.org

worldharvestfaithchurch@gmail.com

Dr. Emita Williams

Graduated Master's Degree Education Administration and a Doctor in Education Leadership,

Dec.2017

She just recently Graduate December 2017 from Maryville University, and received a Master Degree Education Administration and a Doctor in Education Leadership, What inspire her to be a teacher her mother…but she did not want me to be a teacher, she wanted her to be a journalist our a news reporter, but she decided to pursue her dream to be a teacher and attended SIUE and graduated May 1999, with her Bachelors of Science in Early Childhood and May 2009, Maryville University Masters in Early Childhood. She has been teaching for 19 years now, since graduating from SIUE thanks to one of her professors;
Dr. Suzie Nall introduce her to River Garden School District. Her goal now is to become a Principle or Early Child hood education Administration and become a Superintended.

Dr. Emita Williams
"The Power of Focus"

Dr. Emita Williams is a wonderful wife to Mr. Donald Williams and a mother of 7 beautiful children. She has taken on one of her passion in being a, actress in an upcoming Feature film in "Locker Room The Movie". At the age of 42 she always believe you can begin again. I will like to encourage everyone to keep God first you are never too old to fulfill your purpose because God has a plan and he won't you to not leave this earth full of your dream and be led by God.

"God is first, and my family is my second priority"

Dr. Emita believe her friend will say she is a loyal, fun loving person and like to have fun, but most of all put God first. A person of inspiration has been Oprah Winfrey, because she has an awesome testimony that has pushed herself while having a self-driven determination that keep her focus on her career in spite of all the rejection in her life. What has inspired Dr. Emita Williams to pursue her PH D, she always had a plan to pursue greater. She also like to model and be a good role model to younger women and children to help aid in others desires to pursue their dream and goal by showing them how to go after what God has in store for you to be great leaders, to position yourself around like-minded people. You have to keep God first and stay focus on the vision God has given you.

Forever Begins Today!

Evangelist Meishel Matkins

"I Am an Overcomer"

"I Am an Overcomer"

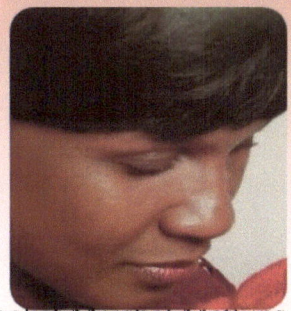

She knew at age 12 she wanted to sing gospel music to the World singing from her heart to God people to hear the voice of God through the music God give her to minister to others heart. Her desire is to travel to minister to God people through music.

Evangelist Meishel Matkins is a native of East St Louis, Illinois, when she was 12 years old walking around singing at her grandmother's house with a broom or brush in her hands. She started singing secular music and start writing song. They did not sound right to her, so she wanted to write gospel songs instead. She said, "she can do anything through Christ that strengthen her." She is into real estate, dreams of owning her own shelter for homeless people, she had to reconnect herself to God instead of doing things her way. She asked God what her purpose was because she felt as she is not she didn't have to be checking and job placement to was just taking a job to live pay check to pay check is not the will of God. She asked God what was her purpose and he told her to open a woman's shelter for mother and children.

Evangelist Meishel Matkins have always been a dreamer in spite her being a battered woman, she is an overcomer. Her heart and desire are to have a battered woman shelter housing for woman and their children, to be able to minister the word of God, help other woman that has been battered, even though there are battered men. The vision God has given her is to help batter women because she can relate to them. Her passion for battered woman to help them know that they are beautiful, and God will give them a safe haven and can overcome any obstacles that tries to stand in their way. Her heart desire is to help aid them to have housing and job placement to make a difference in their life. She has even more dreams to have real estate properties and a Laundromat to be able to accommodate the communities need. Open opportunities and doors to help people of God, because I believe every good dream comes from God. A couple of people she said has inspired her is Mary Mary, Prophetess Shamika Curry, her husband Pastor Joseph M. Curry, Prophetess Margret Green and so many others, if she said you have inspired her she means it.

CALL AND SCHEDULE FOR YOUR EVENT TODAY!!!!
(904) 661-9253

Norma Solano
"Destine for Greatness"

Ms. Norma Solano age 21, been in a movie" Locker Room The Movie" it was such an amazing experience to be working with Mr. Joseph Curry, his lovely wife Shamika and cast.

She has always wanted to be an actress this movie opportunity actual made one of her dreams come true. This is what she always wanted to be in a movie ever since she was a little girl.

Even in her young age she wants to have more opportunity to be on, T.V. shows, travel around the world.

Her project she is trying to accomplish at this moment in her life, she will like to write a book, be a singer and love to learn how to play the guitar. The book she like to write will be about helping teens to be destine for greatness. She will also like to buy her a house to help establish her family stability. She is the 7th out of 8 siblings making her second to the last youngest child.

"Destine for Greatness"

She said her mother and father inspires her to be a better person.

They are very loyal and dedicated parent to their children and to people in general.

She is planning on traveling the world and doing more movies in the future!

Norma Solano said, "Dreams do Come True"

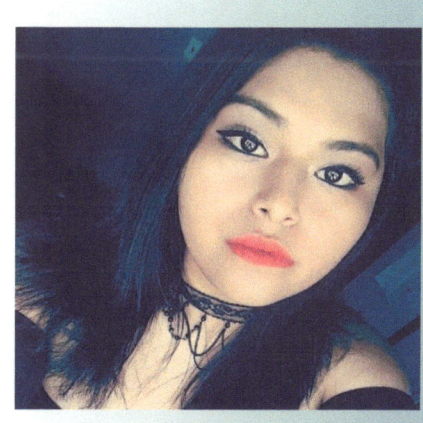

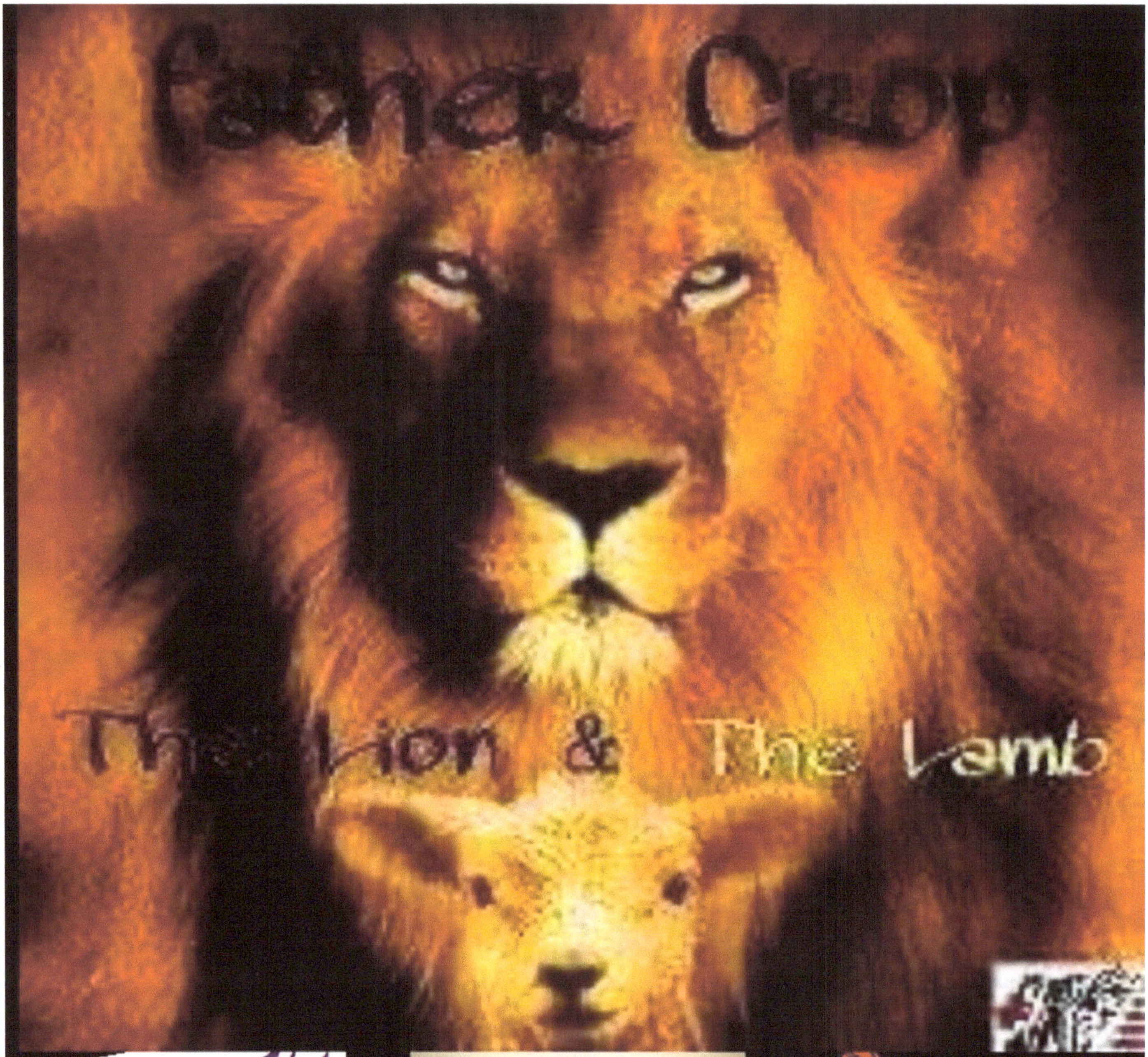

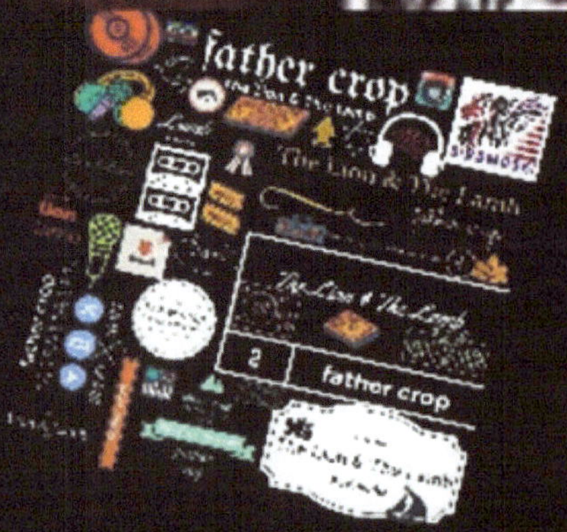

"Father Crop"
DeAndre Thompson
(618) 671-2446
farmerfisherman777@gmail.com

"Don't Work Don't Eat You Go to put in Labor"

DeAndre Thompson "Father Crop" is a native of East St Louis IL, he is a proud father to his son.

He has always been a fan of music, he's old school from the break dance era, beat street and Michael Jackson of the wall beats type of stuff. He has been rapping since 1994, for secular but for as the ministry for the Lord he starts pulling my coat tail to start rapping for Him, he heard it clear as day the Holy Spirit was telling him to rap for God around 1998, so I wrote my first song. Then in 2005 one of the guys he was doing music with pass away, and he was trying to get over a hard grief of his friend, then his brother turns around and got kill. After all the tragedy in his life he ran to the Lord and start been active in church in 2008 he gave his life back to the Lord and start speaking in tongues. He was just trying to get a personal relationship with God, read his Bible, he stops listen to music for a while until one day he was at church he realizes how much he misses rapping. So, he was trying to listen to clean rap music, but they keep taking about money, so he decided to stick to listen to gospel music. Then every blue moon he will listen to the radio and I was into the beat to some of the music, he was like I still want to rap. He started to listen to some inspirational music like; Eazy E, Bone Thugs-N- Harmony and other artist. He started free styling and like the way everything was flowing together so, he goes to get his rap book out, but he said he wanted to start written in his prayer book instead because he is going to rap for the Lord.

Minister for the Lord his names Father Crop was birth at a church he was attending to and a Lady from his church start prayer for him and called him " Father Crop" mantle was birth and ordain through prayer at church, this became his ministry and rap name. The Holy Spirit is the one who inspired him to start rapping again for the Lord. Because he thought rap was corny, until he started rapping and heard other people rap that was not so corny.

In the 80's he used to call this dollar prayer line, they will say a prayer for you and a scripture and a Bible story and then rap at the end. He used to call it every day, he was being train up to be "Father Crop", he was chosen for this, it called him, he did not call it, he chose to be obedient and accept the call from the Lord. Now his music is his therapy.

He came to the Lord because of a crisis, he made his mind up to serve the Lord, and not because his mother told him too. He has more compassion for Gods people because he was rejected, so he wants to be an inspiration to help serve teen, youth and ages twenty and up, need to be cultivated and encourage too. Because some churches treat you like a king and queen until you get a certain age and once the past up the age thirteen and up they start treating you like a heathen once you get in your teens. He said we tend to forget about the Cream of the crop, this will be the middle ages like in their thirties and up. You can't forget about the cream in the middle, that's were the revelation came from about the cream. The Oreo cookie the bottoms is the youth and the top of the cookie is the elders then you have the middle and the middle is the cream,

In the next five years He want to be a better man of God, he wants to be living on all his music and art, he do not want to work for no one else all his life. He wants a barn or a building to be able to help be able to help the community and due their daily teachings, because they are closing all the schools in the city of East St. Louis. That's what Cream Of The Crop is all about help others that might not get an sports academic scholarship, but they are gifted in music and art, he wants a center to be able to help those cultivate their gifts and talents God has given them and keep them out of trouble. The gold and the treasures are in our inner cities. That's why I want to be rich not for fame, but to be able to help impact people lives. He wants a shelter for woman, men and children, to be able to help families, if they need help for skills, rehab, or just a new fresh start of life.

His friends will say he is passion about music and love for his son. It's the Lord and people who inspires him and different artist, He cares and have love for Gods people, to love themselves through the eyes of Christ, never given up on their dreams. Also Tupac was a person that cared about the people and had love for the people, he always quote; Keep your head up! Love yourself so, you can love one another.

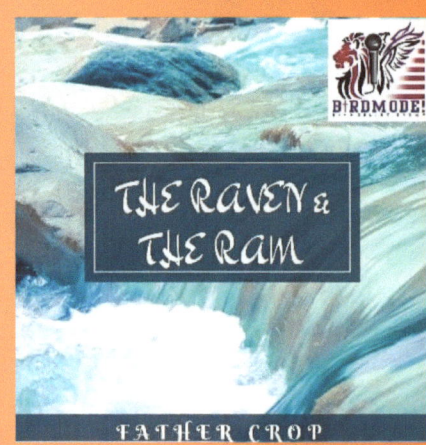

He said he is working on three album projects now in 2018

Cream CR 3 Christ Rule Resurrection,

The Raven and the Ram

Victory Formation

Bird Mode Family Cream of the Crop

"Locker Room The Movie" soundtrack

Contact Information Father Crop

Contact Information Father Crop @birdmodelaborcream@gmail.com (618) 671 - 2446

Better Wear
Custom Apparel

We Give You Best Quality Printing!

1 (618) 560-2015

Facebook & Instagram
@
betterwearcustomapparel

Jhonny Solano
"Design with a Purpose"

Jhonny Solano is 21 years old, he started his business at age 18

"Better Wear Custom Apparel." He started his business in his living room for about 3 months before he opened his own shop in September 2017 that is located 2204 State St. East St Louis IL 62201. He started making t-shirts design in 2014 working for someone else and they pushed him into opening his own shop. He did not like working for minimal wage, and for someone else, so he started his own business. He knew he had a talent that was more valuable, his passion is to customize any clothing, picture, stickers, and family reunions etc.

His dream is to be in movies, a rapper, basketball player and a business owner entrepreneur.

Business has always been in him, at the age of 15 he uses to go and shovel snow, cut grass, just to make a living. Jhonny is inspired by Bill Gates and Elon Musk. He is also the second oldest out of five children.

His five years goals is to be a millionaire, open a franchise for Better Wear Custom Apparel. He has all ways been a risk taker, he is very funny, and a fun person to hang out with.

His plan is to open several businesses to make a difference to help give back to our communities, make a difference in the world, and to make someone happy.

Jhonny Solano believe in giving great customer service, to help express yourself, create expression through your clothing attire, to give you the best quality printing!

Facebook and Instagram@betterwearcustomapparel

"Woman on a Mission from God"
Minister Cynthia Newell

Native of St Louis Mo, she is 41 years young, Author and life coach of R.I.S.E. & W.I.N. Is acronym Release, Internal, Struggle, Effortlessly & Walk in Newness.   She has such a good heart toward Gods people, she ministers to all God's children to support the body of Christ with the gift God has given her to talk to the people to produce eternal healing, to walk in newness of life, giving God the glory in the Kingdom. She has also published three books, first book published 2009, "Oh To Tell The Story" about African American women "This Way to Sunny" collection of love poems, "Gemini Diaries" heart of a woman that captures part of herself as a woman of God spiritual growth evolving in her gift as a Prophetess, a woman going through divorce, single parenthood, getting back in the dating season, remarried and a lot of relating topic. She uses these books as a platform to more intimate conversation open topic and discussion to young men, woman, to help them deeper their spiritual connects to be more empathetic and compassionate towards one another.

She thanks God for putting this on her heart to write poetry this was a way she was able to overcome generation curses on her family battling with

> *"Minister Cynthia is a very funny and life of the party kind of lady"*

addition spirit in her family, this inspired her to start written poetry, because this gave her a voice to express herself even through the loss of her granny mother and cousin. Due to all she has been through she is still focus on the vision God has given her, Titus 2:2 out of this God has birth out another assignment. The Titus 2 Workshop the older woman and younger women. God has given her to reach out to our younger generation to do workshop to help cultivate young girls ages 10 through 16 to help build more confidence and to let them know they are beautiful, and not based on what society think, and stop bullying because when she was young, she was bullied and my daughter was also bullied, so I have such a heart an compassion to help those who has been bullied trying to keep up with today's society. That's why, she has created **Little Sisters Big Vision the will created their vision board God has for them. She also want to work with wise woman they can rise and win**. God has given her more books which is going to be a series "The Day I Found Myself" defining moments as a woman, marriage, ministry etc…..

You can join her, for more information @ www.Cynthiasnewell.com

She has a show online Powerless to Powerful exclusive interview on Every 2nd and 4th Saturday of each month central standard time 1 pm. Pod case lesson of life help other people from feeling powerless to powerful, through the grace of God. its full of love, laughter, support and great

Daring Daughters

Titus 2:2

Minister Cynthia said she inspires herself in spite of all she has been through from God healing her from stage 3 cancer, she never had the backing and support and love she need when life had serve her some tough times. Been homeless twice , divorcee, but in spite of it all she still have love and compassion for God people to still love and do the will of God for her life and destiny.

Her goal this year is to touch and reach

Her goal this year is to touch and reach 100 girls and women are whatever the will of God, He has in store for her.

GEMINI DIARIES
Heart of a Woman

In her latest poetry book, "Gemini Diaries: Heart of a Woman" Cynthia Sherrell masterfully captivates the hearts of readers with secret sentiments about self-image, internal struggles, an expanded view of God & so much more. Available on Amazon.

www.cynthiasnewell.com

CYNTHIA SHERRELL

Place your ad today!

Send information to: vendorsjubileemagazine@gmail.com

TALMAGE CHANDLER
"MORE THAN A CONQUEROR"

TALMAGE CHANDLER 19 YEARS OF AGE AT THIS MOMENT, ATTENDS COLLEGE AT SWIC, (SOUTHWESTERN ILLINOIS COLLEGE) HE WILL BE IN AN UPCOMING FEATURE FILM "LOCKER ROOM THE MOVIE", THAT WILL BE PREMIERING AUGUST 17, 2018. TALMAGE SAID THAT, HE NEVER THOUGHT HE WOULD BE AN ACTOR UNTIL HIS MOTHER INTRODUCE HIM TO THIS MOVIE, HE TRIED IT AND BEGAN TO LOVE ACTING, HE DID NOT KNOW HE HAD IT IN HIM, UNTIL PASTOR CURRY A GREAT DIRECTOR, CULTIVATED HIM TO BRING OUT THE BEST IN HIM.

He never dreamed of being an actor, but after being a part of this feature film he has experience a whole new outlook on acting and began to enjoy acting.

He said his grandmother is the one who inspires him, she has a great heart always put people before herself and very given.

Talmage, has a really good heart, loyal and a great personality, like to make people laugh. He said his grandmother is the one who inspires him.

I ask, Talmage what inspired him the most about being in the movie, he said it's going to be awesome to be seen across the world, plus it was great working with a really cool cast! His next move will be finishing college, traveling, serving our country, going to the air force, getting a house.

Scene from

"Looker Room

The Movie"

Vendors Jubilee

Looking for professional people

Now Hiring

Editors
Journalist
Marketers
Representative
TeleMarketers

Will train, no experience necessary!

Join The Team

Call schedule your interview today!

904 661-9253

VISIT OUR WEBSITE FOR APPLICATION
WWW.VENDORSJUBILEE.COM

"Grace"

Anette Peoples 'Grace ' is a native of St. Louis. Mo. Married to Gerald Peoples and a mother of two beautiful little girls. She is a Christian Lipson, she sings, and raps. She has always been into music, because her mother and father expose and introduce her to different styles of music as a young child, so the passion and love for music was always in her.

Early in her career She said she calls herself Grace because it was birth through prayer and God spoke to her and said Grace. So, when she looks up her name Anette means full of Gods grace and favor. So, she goes by Grace as she ministers to God people.

She is really passion about music and salvation for God people and people in the world not save. God told her to mix together the love of music, by using His Word with her music so a lot of people do not realize they are reciting the scriptures from the Bible through her music. Her passion is to reach the youth, and get wisdom by God, because a lot of youth is into Performing Art.

In 2011 at the age of twenty-one is when she wrote her first song, and now at age thirty-two she continues to write songs and poems. In the next five years she sees herself as a Dr Physical Therapy and to be an Alderwoman of Belleville to really impact our community for the youth, to help improvise professionalism and entrepreneur's in our High School, Grade school and work with youth as an advocate to help cultivate the next generation, so they can have a plan for their future.

Grace friend would say she gets turnt up all the time, get the job done for the Kingdom, a go getter. She is truly an encouraging person. she believes in treating others the way she wants to be treated.

Her other dreams she will like to see is her ministry seeing her music her craft in the next five years and established online, in store, and to do ministry full time and out-music to be more encouraging to can fulfill their dreams. Her Passion do mission and ministry fulltime. established in her life evolving and perfect her music to be more CDs. She would love reach. She wants her people, knowing they is really to travel and

"Let me be a yelling vessel for God to use me for His Glory"

What inspires her the most is herself because when she was going through trials and tribulation I had to encourage myself and said there is someone out there is going through worst than I. and just being save help motive me knowing God has brought me out of situation. So, I want to inspire and help someone else to let them know God will and can bring them out too.

Contact Grace for booking:

Booking Grace5@gmail.com

314 601-5926

Book your next event: Birthday Party., Concert, Church, Mentorship etc.

For Advertising information please contact our Advertising Department @ vendorsjubileemagazine@gmail.com
www.vendorsjubilee.com

Nikki Stewart-Weiss, DC, MS
Doctor of Chiropractic
Nutrition Specialist
Independent Contractor

Phone: 636-379-1779 ext. 1022
Fax: 636-634-3496

Email:
nikki.stewart-weiss@sandhillcounseling.com

801 S. Woodlawn Avenue, Suite 15,
O'Fallon, MO 63366

www.sandhillcounseling.com

Pastor Joseph M. Curry

"Man, with A Vision"

Pastor Joseph M. Curry is a native of East St Louis IL, he is a pastor, writer, and film director and his greatest thing is to be a husband.

He knew he was going to be a pastor when God came to him in a serious of three dreams back to back, the church he went to visit, it was the same church God showed him in his dream. He prayed about it and talk to the pastor of that church and he knew this was the place it was like it felt like fire shut up in his bones like Jeremiah. He felt like Jonah in the dream. God inspired him to write books, he said God is the Author and he just the tool God use to write his books it's a message God wanted his people to hear. He said he's not superman, the Bible said in Philippians 4:13 "I can do all this through him who gives me strength." He wants to least reach one soul at a time for the Kingdom of God.

The projects he is working on now, he has so much on his plate after finishing "Locker Room The Movie". Waiting on the world premiere of this feature film. He is working on his seventh book, comic book and more feature films.

His focus is to go out and deliver God people, he feels like he is a beacon of light for God to go and help delivered God people from demonic bondage. God has given him some effective tools in his books. "Breakthrough into your Victory," Under Construction God is Rebuilding Men," Getting in Shape with God A Spiritual Workout," Clocking in for the Kingdom of God," Breaking the Chains of Demonic Bondage," and Coffee House Christian." Sounds funny but it's reality.

With all the work he has accomplish its harvest time, because these are seed that's has been planted. God has put him in his field to tend his Gardener, that s his desire. God has put him he his Spiritual garden to tend it for him.

He wrote this movie while driving to Iowa to get his daughter from college on the High thinking and not knowing it was going to be a movie.

"Pastor, Author, Visionary"

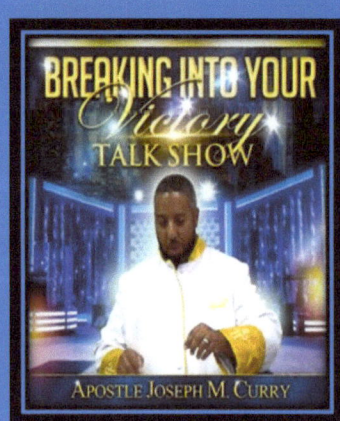

Christian Film Diector: "Locker Room The Movie

It's really dealing with a young man and teens dealing with anger, rebellion, religions, bullying atheists and every aspect of life. This movie is going to reach multi culture. The devil doesn't pick color he wants souls. It doesn't matter what color you are, God created us in his image, it's not about the color of your skin it's about you are in the Kingdome of God.

Mr. Curry think he is truly a comedian who like to make people smile and put a smile on people face. Who is a very loving being and who is a chef and loves to cook. His desire is to reach and help save as many people God has in store for him to reach for the Kingdom of God.

He has accomplished many dreams God has given him but the most accomplishment of them all is to save soul. He said he believe he is the Hulk to break every spiritual bondage from God people sometimes he feels that the weight is on his shoulders, so he had to learn to turn it over to God. He said the people in his life inspires him first his wonderful wife really encourages him she is my rib, son, daughters, mother, his family without them and God he would be nothing.

You can purchase all his books on any online book store.

"Her future goal is to go to college, start her on business, home realtor, and an entrepreneur".

Casey Howliet
"Pursuing Your Destiny"

Casey Howliet age 19 a native from O'Fallon IL, she has always been a part of the theater in High School, never dream of being an actress and auditioning for "Locker Room The Movie" really took her out of her comfort zone, but the experience was well worth it. In spite having to learn the script had its challenges, but she pursues and was determining to perfect her role in this movie.

Her future goal is to go to college, start her on business, home realtor, and an entrepreneur.

"Locker Room The Movie" Coming soon to a theatre near you!

At this moment she is working at a daycare, her passion come from her uncle and grandmother to be an entrepreneur. They have been very positive role model in her life, encouraging her to finish school to be a positive role model to her peers.

She is planning on finishing her some online college course, traveling and pursuing more acting opportunities. Go check her out "Locker Room The Movie" coming soon to a theater near you!

(On the set of "Locker Room The Movie")

Lyric Chantel
"Destine to Win"

Lyric Chantel 18 years of age a native form Belleville IL, been a cheerleader all her life. Always been into hair make up and at this moment in cosmetology school. Her dream is to build her on brand and image sell hair, be a barber, on clothing line and new fragrance, always wanted to be an actress.

Her friends told her they were casting for Locker Room The Movie, so she audition and go the part. She always wanted to be in a movie and always knew it was destining to happen. Accepting this actress role for this movie has taught me a lot of dos and don'ts when it comes to filming, like looking at the camera and really becoming the character I was acting I had to learn how to become that character at that moment and not just act it out.

I have always wanted to be an actress and model, people would always say I am a drama queen, always have something to say, very opinionated and bold.

"Gabrielle Union, Taraji P. Henson are a great inspiration to her because they are independent and a very strong black role models. She also admires Snoop Dog, because he so laid back and always giving to the communities".

I LOVE FASHION, DURING HAIR, AND KEEPING MY NAILS DONE!

Her future goal is to do modeling shows, focus on her hairline, and hopefully do part 2 for Locker Room The Movie.

Her friend will say she is very loud, opinionated, out spoken, bold, funny and goofy.

She said Gabrielle Union, Taraji P. Henson are a great inspiration to her because they are independent and a very strong black role models. She also admires Snoop Dog, because he so laid back and always giving to the communities.

Her new project she is focusing on is being a model and her hairline and she said go check her out in Locker Room The Movie coming soon August 17, 2018.

(Scene from "Locker Room The Movie")

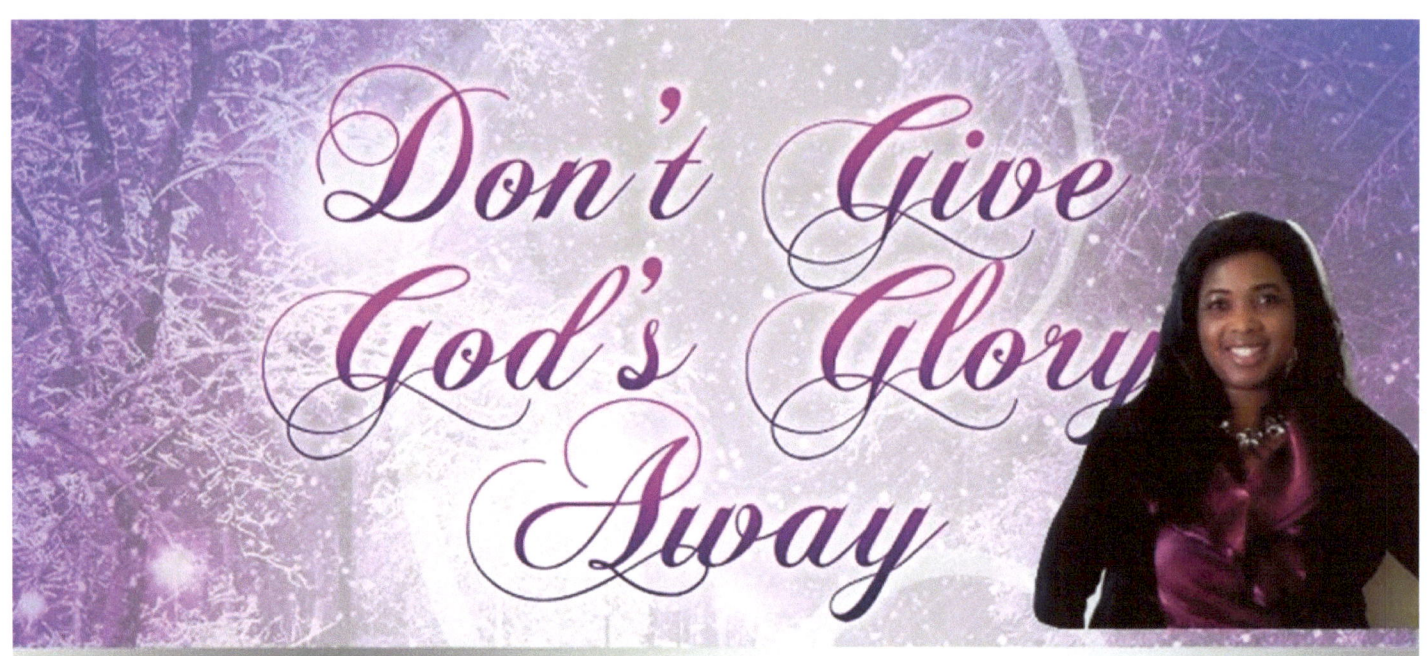

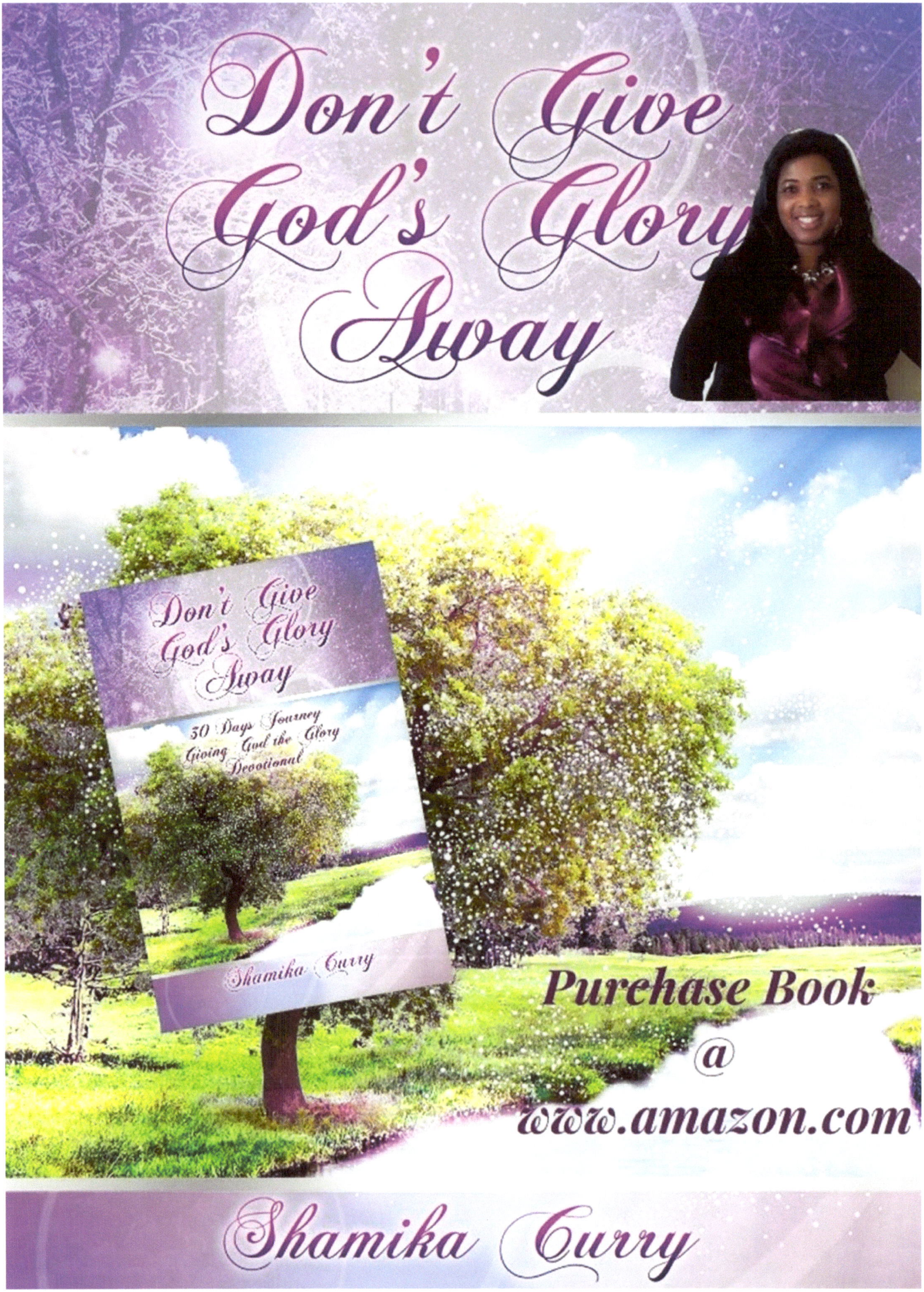
Don't Give God's Glory Away
Don't Give God's Glory Away
30 Days Journey Giving God the Glory Devotional
Shamika Curry
Purchase Book
@
www.amazon.com
Shamika Curry

Look out World

Model

Dezjah

Young Atlanta Fashion Show 2018

Need a Stylish contact Anecia Coleman

618 593=8550

FOR YOUR FASHION, MODELING OR WORDROBE

For more Information, Please Contact necipoohzboutique@gmail.com

Coming soon 2018

"SONG BIRD"

Terianna Brooks

"Truth Be Told" Cd Coming Soon, with her debut single "Truth is The Light"

Coming Soon 2018

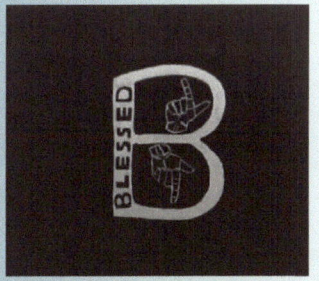

Bless it Up!

William Davis is the founder and Ceo for Bless.Co Clothing line, location in Belleville IL, He started his business at the age of seventeen years of age. He is a native from East St. Louis IL, wasn't going the right way, after losing his father at the age of ten, he was a daddy's boy, he turned to gang's street violence hanging with the wrong people, never though he was going to live to see the age of 18 due to the rough neighborhood and lifestyle he grew up in. Once he made it to eighteen years of age he felt so blessed, made a hands logo, what must go up, must come down, basically that mean what ever happen just put your trust in God. As He grew older at age twenty-one he started making his on clothing line and to continue growing from there. He designs his clothing line to reach everyone who wants to be a blessing and be blessed by God. Bless.co is more of a vision to represent you, once you put this clothing on or hear about it, you should be blessed and brings you happiness, motivation and dedication to your dreams. With the hands everything comes up or down

no matter, a good day or bad day you should sent blessing up to God and blessing will come back down to you.

In the next five year he sees himself open up online store open and donation giving back to his community. He will be coming out with clothing line for male and female major jump new design tank tops, shorts, hats, athlete wear, key chains, cup and more items.

He is a person of business always trying to make money to help make other people dreams come true.

He said everyone inspires him all the people, he has lost his grandmother, his best friend and other people that has died due to cancer, law enforcement. or sickness, so I want to bless it up for them, by showing their vision through me that make me want to do better, by accomplishing store front businesses, to be known by leaving a legacy. He said leaving a legacy is better than being rich. Want everyone to know Bless.Co is a business within it self wants them to know that his business was crested to bless others.

"You wear it you will be Bless"

Contact (618) 301-2869

William Davis

Ceo, Bless.Co

"Dancing is my Passion"

Morgan Elsaw is an eleven year old native from Belleville IL, daughter of proud parents Shauntez & Yvonne Elsaw

She has been in love with dancing ever since she was four years of age. She knew her passion for dancing at an early age, she use to dance in the mirror and all around the house. She has been dancing for seven years now and currently attending Elite Dance Academy in O'Fallon IL. She has always been so passionate about dancing, so her parents enrolled her into Grand Center Arts Academy is St Louis Mo. Is a performing art school that offers dance, theater, and arts, but she is only interested in dance.

Her goal in life is to have plenty of education, to go to college to continue to pursue her dreams in dancing. She wants to be a professional teacher and to be an instructor, to help educate others about dancing.

Her current project she is involve with is a dance group called Lou Kids Gigs Performers, they dance at different sports events, commercials and charity events in Belleville IL.

Her friends will say she is a very caring person. Respectful, fun, happy and treat others the way she wants to be treated.

Who inspires her is mother, father, Coach Mrs. Tanya Reed, family and Mrs. Cooper and any other dancers really inspires her too.

Contact information

@cmore@dancer_morglan

mordancsprkl2024@gmail.com

D'Andre Coleman" Brother Dre", a native of East St. Louis IL, he is a MC, Hip Hop rap artist and does open mic for churches, ever since he was twelve years of age. He started

Christian rap when he was about twenty-five years of age.

He has always been a fan of music, music has been a part of him. Music was never a career it was more like a hobby for him. He started written music at a very young age.

he The name Brother Dre originated when he was doing an open mic night event at a church, it was another young man there and his name was Deandre too, so they introduce him as Brother Dre so he stayed true to that name.

"Don't Lean to your own Understanding, Keep your Head Up"

He started written music mental struggle and tian aspect and speak on tian, to let them know in honor of every young black man doubts; he wanted to apply Christian the journey of your walk as a Christian everyone's walk is different.

Through his music he er people know if you are are not alone, everyone want it to be therapy and to let other going through a mental struggle you has experience some type of

struggle in their life, but God is faithful to bring you out.

His five year goal is to develop more music and artists, dropping a new demo in August, 2018 mix tape" Underground Gospel The Road is Narrow". At age thirty-two, Brother Dre friends will say he is one of a kind, He keeps it real.

He remembers when he was younger how music ministered to him and he want to minister to others through music, being a positive influence that will help an change someone way of thinking through Christian Hip Hop Rap.

His mother is a great inspiration in his life, because she showed him and cultivated his character for life.

"Keep East St. Louis" For Life

Bookings Contact :: neighborhoodmusic618@gmail.com

 Brother Dre 618

Model

Anecia Coleman

Class of 2018

Triumph Woman

Free Open to the Public!

Ladies Join Prophetess Shamika Curry, for an Inspirational Word/Book fellowship gathering. As we come together to help, and be each other strength, as we pursue this daily walk with the Lord!

Monday's

12:00pm or 6:00pm

S.T.R.E.N.G.T.H.

Strong, Triumph, Righteousness, Encourage, Necessary, Guidence, True, Holiness

Come let your hair down, to be healed, uplifted, strengthen, delivered and walk in liberty.

If you like to come Fellowship please reply yes to:

triumphwoman2@gmail.com

Romans 8:37
No, in all these things we are more than conquerors through him who loved us

Refreshments will be serve!

COMING SOON

AUGUST 17, 2018

Locker Room
THE MOVIE

Party Time

- Birthday Parties
- Baby Shower
- Bridal Shower
- Tea Party
- Wedding
- Special Occasion's

Contact: Mrs. Shamika Curry & Staff

Mystiquee Agency Events

mystiqueeagencyevents@gmail.com

904 661-9253

Pageants Commercial Magazine

Mystiquee Agency

Where you are the Star

Model Search

Illinois
Atlanta
Dallas Texas
Orlando Florida
Fashion Show

Ages 5 - 40

Model the light of the World

Send profile to:
mystiqueeagencyevents@gmail.com

Thank You

For Your Support

Contact

Mystiquee Agency

For your next events!

mystiqueeagencyevents@gmail.com

CZG
CROSS GRAIN
APPEARL

CHONSTEN JENNINGS

CGA PRESENTS

CZG
CROSS GRAIN
APPEARL
Young Greatness

SATURDAY, JUNE 30TH FROM 7:30-9PM

VENDOR EXPO AND FASHION SHOW WITH LIVE PERFORMANCES AND MUCH MORE. DON'T WANT TO MISS IT!

DESIGNERS, MAKEUP ARTIST, ART, MUSIC ALL IN ONE!

$7 ONLINE, $10 AT THE DOOR.
EARLY BIRD 15$

COME SUPPORT THESE YOUNG ENTREPRENEURS IN THEIR JOURNEY TO GREATNESS!
GET YOUR TICKETS NOW AT: HTTPS://WWW.EVENTBRITE.COM/O/CROSSGRAIN-APPEARL-17092261934
CONTACT: 407-285-4221
8010 SUNPORT DR SUITE 114, ORLANDO, FL 32809

CGAPPEARL@GMAIL.COM OR 407 285-4221

Hello Business owners, Community leaders, Pastors or ministries! Our company personally extend this great opportunity to ensure growth with in your establishment, by placing a ad in our magazine? I will like to set up a date and time with you to come interview you, for our magazine if interested.

You can make your payment today, and select which ad you are interested in advertising.

Business Card $50
5 7 ad $75
1\2 page $100
8 10 plus interview $150

Magazine will come out every three months

This is a global magazine, that will be place through out our communites in which you live in Just to name a few, Beauty/Barber Salón, Doctors offices, community events, Libraries and any online book stores.

Please send inquires to www.vendorsjubilee.com vendorsjubileemagazine@gmail.com
or call 904 661-9253
To place your order!
If you have any questions please do not hesitate to call.

Thank you
God bless you

www.ingramcontent.com/pod-product-compliance
Lightning Source LLC
Chambersburg PA
CBHW051215220526
45473CB00003B/1035